Robbie Williams
Escapology

How Peculiar

Words & Music by Robert Williams & Guy Chambers.

(Ooh.)

How pec-u-liar. Je - sus what am I to do man, I am a de-pressed man. Not sure what I'm

10

doing all of the day._____ How pec - u - liar._____

I am all of the a -

- bove man, I have what you want man. If you want me

here I am. Come and get it ba - by, oh!

Feel

Words & Music by Robert Williams & Guy Chambers.

My head speaks_ a lan - guage_
be - fore I've__ ar - rived,_____

I don't un - der - stand.__
I can see my - self com - ing.

I just wan - na

feel_____ real__ love,__ feel the home that I live__ in.

'Cause I got too much life_____ run - ning through my veins__

I just wan - na

feel_____ real___ love,___ feel the home that I live___ in.

Something Beautiful

Words & Music by Robert Williams & Guy Chambers.

find that love, it won't leave___ you, may you find it by the end of___ the day,___

___ you won't be lost, hurt, tired___ and lone - ly, some - thing

beau - ti - ful will come your___ way.___ You won't be lost,___ hurt,

tired___ and lone - ly, some - thing beau - ti - ful will come your___ way.___

Monsoon

Words & Music by Robert Williams & Guy Chambers.

1. I've sung some songs that were lame,___ I've slept with girls on the game.
(2.) To all you Sharon's and Mi-chelle's with all your tales to sell,

I've got my Ca-tho-lic shame, Lord I'm in pur-ga-tory
save your meat mo-ney well, I'm glad that spend-ing a

ba-sic-ally, it's all come___ on top___ for me.
night with me guar-an-teed you ce-le-bri-ty.

-room_____ mon - soon,_____

come soon._____

1. F

2. Don't wan - na piss on your_ pa - rade,_ I'm here to make mo - ney and get laid.

Yeah I'm a star but I'll_ fade if you ain't stick - ing_ your knives in me, you will be_ ev-

29

I smoked too ma-ny ci-gar-ettes___ I've had more blondes than bru-nettes,

I'm not ex-pect-ing___ your sym - pa-thy, but it's all been___ too

much for me. So put your hands a - cross the wa-

-ter mush - room,_____ mon -

Sexed Up

Words & Music by Robert Williams & Guy Chambers.

2.

Screw you, I did - n't like_ your taste,_ a - ny - way,

I chose you and that's all gone to waste. It's Sa - tur - day,_ I'll go_ out

and find a - no - ther you._

Why don't we... Why don't we

D.S. al Coda

Love Somebody

Words & Music by Robert Williams & Guy Chambers.

sha- dow on the pave - ment, the dark side of the sun.___ Got a
min- utes in an hour___ or hours in the day.___ A

dream the dream all ov - er and sleep it tight.___ You don't
song played in a cir - cle and that nev- er skips a beat.___ A

wan- na sing the blues___ in black and white.___ And it's
stran- ger in a coun- try that I have yet to meet. And let's

hope that springs e- ter- nal for ev- 'ry - one.___ If
hope that springs e- ter- nal for ev- 'ry - one.___ Your

Revolution

Words & Music by Robert Williams & Guy Chambers.

1. Don't fight the feel-ing, re-lax,___ oh, child, the knots are in your back__

'cause you've been hold - ing on, I feel you when you're reach - ing out.

I'll talk you through me - mo - ries, just keep breath - ing with me.

It's time to hold my hand and walk in - to the re - vo - lu -

- tion. When there's no one to touch and you've been think - ing too
2. When love ling - ers on you're just feel - ing it wrong.

Handsome Man

Words & Music by Robert Williams, Guy Chambers & Adrian Deevoy.

50

graph, though it's not for me.___

Grip and grin, shake and fake, name and shame then I'm out of here.

It's not ve - ry com - pli - ca - ted, I'm just young and ov - er - ra - ted.

Guitar

Ooh!

Please don't drop_ me, I'll fall to pie - ces on__ ya.

If you don't see_ me   I don't ex - ist.   It's nice to   meet you
2° need

now let me go___and wash my hands___   here be- fore you stands.
2° now let me see___ a   show of hands

___   'cause you just met___   the world's most hand - some man.___

The world's most hand - some man.___   The world's most hand - some man.___

___   The world's most hand - some man.

Come Undone

Words & Music by Robert Williams, Boots Ottestad, Ashley Hamilton & Daniel Pierre.

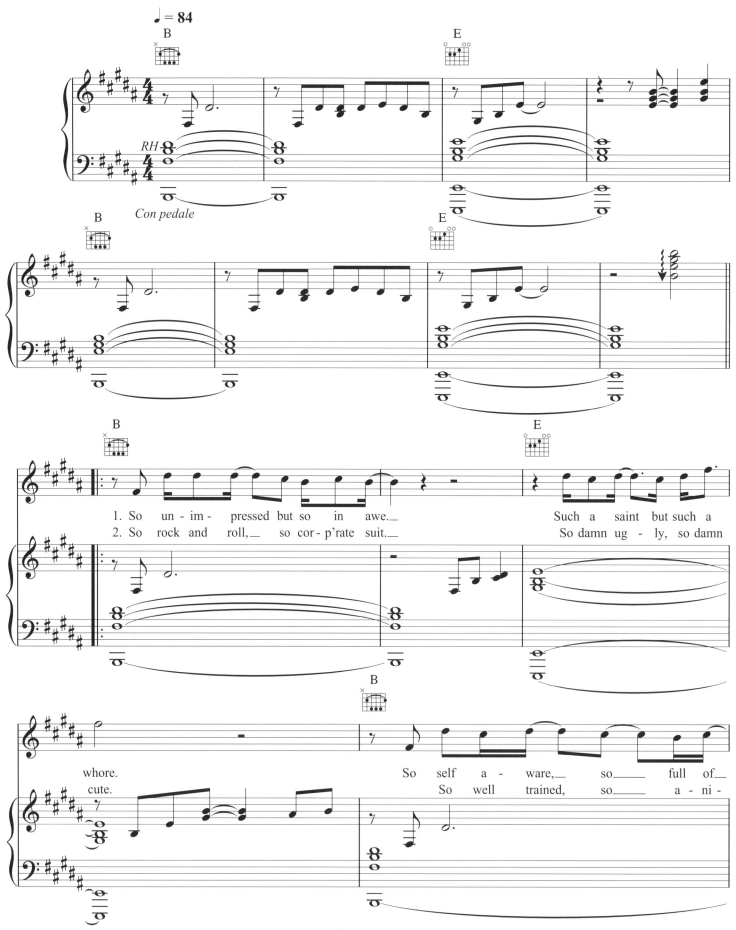

1. So un-im-pressed but so in awe.___ Such a saint but such a
2. So rock and roll,___ so cor-p'rate suit.___ So damn ug-ly, so damn

whore. So self a-ware,___ so___ full of
cute. So well trained, so___ a-ni-

Pray___ that when I'm com - ing down___ you'll be a - sleep.___

If I ev - er hurt___ you your re - venge___ will be___ so sweet, be - cause___ I'm

scum and I'm your___ son.___ I come un - done.___

I come un - done._____

59

love___ songs, so sin - cere.___

so sin - cere.

They're sell - ing ra - zor blades and mir - rors in___ the street.___

Me and My Monkey

Words & Music by Robert Williams & Guy Chambers.

pace."

And when we___ hit the strip___ with all___ the
For - ty min - utes la - ter___ there came a

wed - ding cha - pels and the ne - on signs___ he said "I___
knock at the door.___ In walked this

left my wal - let in El___ Se - gon - do" and pro - ceed - ed to take
big bad ass ba - boon in - to my bed - room___ with three___

two grand of mine.___
mon - key whores.___

"Hi!___ My name is Sun -

Asked the bell boy if he'd take me and my
Was dig - gin' the old Kurt Co - bain sing-ing 'bout

mon - key as well.___ He looked in the pas - sen - ger seat of my
li - thi - um.___ There came a knock at the door

car and with a smile___ he___ said___
and in walked Sun - shine.___ "What's up?

"If your_ mon - key's got that_ kind of mo - ney sir then we've
You'd bet - ter__ get your ass in here boy, your mon-key's hav - ing too much

a - mi - gos, and now your mon - key's__ gon - na die!"_____

Me and my mon - key drove in search of the

sun. Now me and my mon - key, we don't wan -

- na kill__ no Mex - i - can__ but we've got ten itch - y fin -

Looks like we got ourselves a Mexican stand-off here boy and I ain't about to run.

Put your gun down boy.

How'd I get mixed up with this fuckin' monkey anyhow?

74

Hot Fudge

Words & Music by Robert Williams & Guy Chambers.

78

81

Song 3

Words & Music by Robert Williams & Guy Chambers.

1. Come join the band,__ come shag the damned.__
2. So E-bay ba - by, have-n't seen you late -

You've been gloat - ing late - ly ba - by, and I dig L. A.

D.S. al Coda

I'd have to say.____

Coda

U. S. A.____ U. S. A.____ U. S. A.

89

Cursed

Words & Music by Robert Williams, Guy Chambers & Adrian Deevoy.

flirt with dan - ger and a - ny stran - ger.
(thought you'd like it, knew you would - n't de - ny it.)

You're not___ as spu - pid as___ I look.
Saint Pe - ter's gon - na be un - faith - ful,

Be - fore I___ could read___ you wrote___ the book.
tell God he's got a dir - ty an - gel.

Cursed, since your birth___

Hush, ba - by sleep now. We all

miss you, we al - ways will.

Nan's Song

Words & Music by Robert Williams.

1. You said when you'd die that you'd walk with me ev-e-ry___ day.___ And

near,_____ bring - ing hea - ven down__ here._____
2° bring your

2. I miss your

You taught me kings and queens___ while

stroking my hair. In my darkest hour

I know you are there

kneeling down beside me, whispering my

prayer. Yes, there's a strange kind of light

And say was-n't life____ sweet. Then we'll pre - pare

to take hea - ven down____ there.____

Music arrangements by Derek Jones.
Music Processed by Paul Ewers Music Design.
Music edited by Lucy Holliday.

Cover/back cover photography by Lusi Sanchis.
Booklet photography Hamish Brown
Cover design Tom Hingston Studio.
Printed in the United Kingdom by
Caligraving Limited, Thetford, Norfolk.

Published 2002
© International Music Publications Limited
Griffin House, 161 Hammersmith Road,
London W6 8BS, England